Exploring Space

By Gregory Vogt

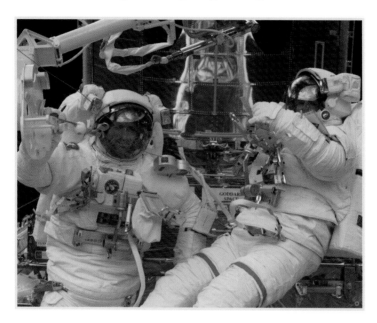

OUR UNIVERSE

www.raintreepublishers.co.uk
Visit our website to find out more information about Raintree books.

To order:
 Phone 44 (0) 1865 888112
 Send a fax to 44 (0) 1865 314091
Visit the Raintree Bookshop at www.raintreepublishers.co.uk to browse our catalogue and order online.

First published in Great Britain by Raintree Publishers, Halley Court, Jordan Hill, Oxford OX2 8EJ, part of Harcourt Education.
Raintree is a registered trademark of Harcourt Education Ltd.

Design: Jo Hinton-Malivoire and Tinstar Design (www.tinstar.co.uk), Jo Sapwell (www.tipani.co.uk)
Illustrations: Art Construction
Picture Research: Maria Joannou and Su Alexander
Production: Jonathan Smith

Originated by Dot Gradations Ltd
Printed and bound in Hong Kong and China by South China Printing

ISBN 1 844 21419 2
07 06 05 04 03
10 9 8 7 6 5 4 3 2 1

British Library Cataloguing in Publication Data
Vogt, Gregory
  1.Outer space – Exploration – Juvenile literature
  I.Title
  523.1

A full catalogue record for this book is available from the British Library.

Acknowledgements
Cover Photo:
All photographs courtesy of NASA.

Content consultant
David Jewitt
Professor of Astronomy
University of Hawaii Institute for Astronomy.

Every effort has been made to contact copyright holders of any material reproduced in this book. Any omissions will be rectified in subsequent printings if notice is given to the publishers.

Any words appearing in the text in bold, **like this**, are explained in the glossary.

flight deck
where the pilot
operates the
space shuttle
controls

cargo bay
where objects
that the space
shuttle carries
into space are
kept

spacelab
a laboratory
where
astronauts do
experiments

main engines
rockets that fire
on lift-off
to help push
the shuttle
into space

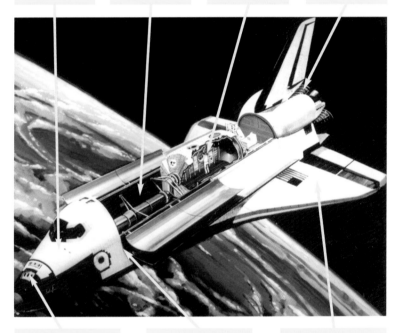

small rockets
to help the shuttle
move and change
its path

lower deck
where the
astronauts
live and work

wings
parts the shuttle uses
to glide through the
Earth's atmosphere
to its landing site

A quick look at space exploration

How do people travel into space?
People travel in spacecraft that are pushed into space by powerful rockets.

What types of spacecraft do astronauts ride in?
Today, most astronauts travel into space in space shuttles. These reuseable spacecraft look like aeroplanes.

How do people survive in space?
Spacecraft supply astronauts with air, food and other things necessary to survive.

How do astronauts survive outside spacecraft?
Astronauts wear spacesuits when they leave their spacecraft. The spacesuit protects them from deadly energy waves in space. It also keeps them warm. Tanks on the back of the suit provide air for astronauts to breathe.

What other worlds have people visited?
People have landed on the Moon, but they have not yet visited any other planets.

These rockets are pushing a spacecraft into space.

Rocket power

For thousands of years, people have wondered what other worlds in space are like. Some people in ancient times dreamed of exploring space, but they had no way of travelling there.

Rocket technology was invented in China in about AD 1100. Early Chinese rockets were made from bamboo tubes. The front end of the tube was closed, and the back end was open. The open end of the tube was filled with gunpowder. The gunpowder was lit to fire the rocket. This caused a small explosion. The force of the explosion pushed the rocket upwards.

Over the years, people have found many uses for rockets. Rockets carry fireworks into the air. During a war, people use rockets to carry weapons. Powerful rockets can now carry machines and people into space.

About space rockets

Today, scientists use rockets to travel into space. The basic rocket for space travel is a long tube with a pointed front end. The pointed design improves the way the rocket travels through the air.

Rocket engines are at the bottom end of the tube. Early rockets had one engine. Modern rockets have three or more engines.

Some rockets have stabilizers. Stabilizers are wings shaped like fins on the bottom of the rocket. Stabilizers help balance the rocket.

Rockets carry things like **satellites** and space capsules into space. A satellite is a spacecraft that circles the Earth. A space capsule is a small bell-shaped spacecraft. The machines and equipment rockets carry are called payloads.

Fuel is stored inside the rocket tube. Rocket engines can run on several types of fuel. Early rockets used solid fuel, such as gunpowder. Modern rockets use liquid fuel, such as liquid oxygen and liquid **hydrogen**. Some rockets use more than one kind of fuel. Using a combination of different fuels gives the rocket more power.

During blast-off the fuel is ignited, or set on fire, to power the rocket engines. This causes flames and gas from the engines to rush out of nozzles, or tubes,

▲ **This is a photo of a space shuttle blasting off into space.**

at the bottom end of the rocket. The very, very hot gases speed out and push against the ground. This pushes the rocket upwards.

Rockets blast off from a launch pad. A launch pad is an area away from people and buildings. The noise from a rocket launch could damage people's hearing. People should also stay far away in case accidents happen or faulty rockets explode.

▲ **Rockets need a great deal of thrust to push spacecraft into space.**

Why rockets work

Rocket designs are based on the three laws of motion. The English scientist Sir Isaac Newton was the first to state these laws in 1687.

The first law says that an object's motion remains constant, or the same. What this means is that a moving object keeps moving until something else stops it. Something that is sitting still stays still unless an outside force pushes it and puts it in motion. A rocket needs the force produced by its engines to lift it.

The second law says that every action has an equal and opposite reaction. For example, the gases from the burned fuel shoot downwards out of the end of a rocket. This action creates an opposite reaction. The fuel's downward force pushes the rocket upwards.

The third law says that the greater the force, the more an object will move. It also explains that a heavier object needs greater force to move it. For example, if a person pushes an empty swing gently, the swing does not move much. But if the person pushes harder, the swing moves more. The person must push even harder if someone is sitting on the swing.

Rockets use fuel to push themselves upwards. They burn a great deal of fuel very quickly. Gas and fire speed out of nozzles at the bottom of the rocket. This creates a lot of force called thrust. Thrust pushes rockets upwards very quickly.

Rockets need greater thrust when they carry heavy payloads into space. The heavier the payload, the greater the thrust needed to send it into space. Scientists may use large rockets or several rockets at one time to create more thrust.

more power. He also believed liquid-fuelled rockets could travel all the way to the Moon.

Goddard made a rocket with an upside-down design. The engine was at the top and pointed downwards. He made a fuel tank to hold liquid fuel and attached it to the bottom of the engine. Based on Newton's second law of motion, the force flowing out of the bottom of the engine would push the rocket up.

Goddard fired his first rocket in 1926. It climbed to 18 metres. Goddard then improved his rocket design. Some of his rockets climbed thousands of metres. Today, liquid fuel is used in most rockets that fly into space.

Stages

Scientists build modern rockets in parts called stages. Each stage falls away when it is no longer needed. This makes the rocket lighter, so the engines in the remaining stages can make it go even faster.

Most rockets have a three-stage design. The first stage lifts the rocket from the ground. It falls off when it runs out of fuel. The second stage carries the rocket higher into the **atmosphere**. The second stage also falls off when it runs out of fuel. Then the third stage takes the rocket into space.

This picture was taken from the inside of a space shuttle while it was in space. It shows the cargo bay where the payload is kept.

Missiles and spacecraft

The first rockets to be fired into space were missiles. A missile is a long rocket that carries a weapon on its front end. Scientists design missiles to be aimed at enemy targets. To reach its target, the missile travels very high above the Earth in a curved path. At the top of the curve, the missile begins to travel down towards its target.

Scientists realized that missiles could also be used for travelling through space. During their early space

Astronauts on board

The first manned spacecraft was *Vostok 1*, launched by the Soviet Union in April 1961. It carried Yuri Gagarin into space. Later space capsules, like the USA's *Gemini*, carried more astronauts. The *Apollo* capsule (above) held three astronauts. The *Space Shuttle Orbiter* can hold up to eight astronauts. The *Orbiter* is like an aeroplane. Two rockets sit on both sides of the *Orbiter* and push it into space. The *Space Shuttle Orbiter* was the first reusable spacecraft.

programmes, the USA and the **Soviet Union** used missiles to carry payloads into space.

Missiles carried the first satellites into **orbit** around the Earth. Satellites have many uses. They gather information, send information and take pictures.

Missiles also launched the first astronauts into space. Up to three astronauts sat inside a space capsule. The rocket pushed the capsule into space. When it returned to the Earth, the capsule parachuted to Earth or splashed down into the ocean. A ship was sent to pick up the astronauts.

Scientists still use missiles to send spacecraft into space, but astronauts now ride inside space shuttles instead of capsules. The space shuttle is a reusable aeroplane-like spacecraft designed for astronauts.

▲ This is an artist's drawing of *Mariner 2*. It was one of the first spacecraft to fly past a planet.

Early space missions

The first ever space probe was *Luna 1*, launched by the **Soviet Union** in January 1959. *Luna 1* passed the Moon and then continued into space. Three years later the USA's National Aeronautics and Space Administration (NASA) launched *Mariner 2*. *Mariner 2*'s mission was to travel to Venus to study the planet. At the time, no space probe had ever visited Venus.

The *Mariner 2* space probe flew over 40 million kilometres (26 million miles), travelling past Venus at a distance of about 35,000 kilometres (22,500 miles).

Mariner 2 was one of the first spacecrafts to successfully reach another planet. It measured Venus's temperature, studied Venus's clouds and measured other things about the planet. *Mariner 2* proved that unmanned machines could be space explorers.

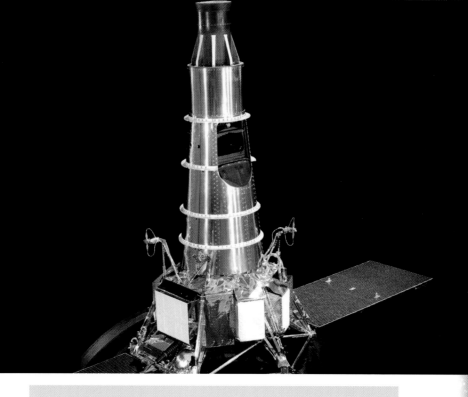

▲ **This is an artist's drawing of a *Ranger*. Before it crashed, it took pictures of the Moon.**

Going to the Moon

One of the early goals of the US and Soviet space programmes was to send humans to the Moon. The Moon is a rocky ball that is 3475 kilometres (2160 miles) in diameter. Diameter is the distance from one side of a sphere or circle to the other. The Moon is around 384,400 kilometres (238,800 miles) from the Earth.

Planning the Moon mission was difficult. Scientists knew the journey to the Moon would be long and dangerous. Astronauts would have to travel many thousands of kilometres to get there. They would be in space for a week or more, and they would need a way to land on the Moon.

Astronauts would also need spacesuits to protect themselves on the Moon's surface. Spacesuits keep an astronaut's body at the right temperature. The suit's fabric protects the body from the Sun's harmful rays. Tanks on the back of the suit provide oxygen for the astronaut to breathe.

Scientists did not know if conditions on the Moon were dangerous. Some people thought there might be huge pools of dust like quicksand. So scientists sent spacecraft to the Moon before the astronauts went.

Beginning in the late 1950s, three different kinds of spacecraft went to the Moon. *Ranger* spacecraft carried television cameras. The cameras took close-up pictures of the Moon's surface and sent them back to the Earth. The pictures showed no liquid water on the Moon. Instead, dust-like soil and light grey and black rocks covered the ground.

Surveyor spacecraft had rocket engines and legs. They landed on the Moon and did not find any dust pools.

Lunar Orbiters circled the Moon. They took pictures of possible landing sites for the astronauts.

 Apollo **astronauts put a US flag on the Moon when they landed.**

Apollo missions

Apollo was the name of the US space programme in charge of sending astronauts to the Moon. NASA scientists designed special spacecraft for these missions. Each *Apollo* spacecraft had two parts.

The first part was a command module. This is where the astronauts lived. It was built to stay in **orbit** around the Moon and then return to the Earth.

The second part was the lander. It had four legs and a large engine for landing. While in space, the lander was attached to the command module. It separated from the module to land on the Moon.

People first landed on the Moon during the *Apollo 11* mission. Three astronauts rode in a capsule at the top of the world's largest rocket. Their names were Neil Armstrong, Michael Collins and Edwin Aldrin, Jr.

On 16 July 1969, *Apollo 11* launched from the Kennedy Space Centre in Florida. *Apollo 11* travelled for three days before it entered the Moon's orbit. Then Armstrong and Aldrin climbed into the lander. Collins stayed in the command module above the Moon. On 20 July 1969, Armstrong and Aldrin landed on the Moon.

Accidents

Spacecraft are built to high safety standards. Unfortunately, accidents can still happen. In January 1986, the *Challenger* space shuttle exploded as it launched into space, killing seven astronauts. In February 2003, the *Columbia* space shuttle exploded as it re-entered the Earth's atmosphere. A further seven astronauts lost their lives.

Astronauts know there is a risk when they travel into space. They take this risk to help the people on the Earth find out more about our universe.

Mariner 10 to Venus and Mercury

One of the great, early explorer space probes was *Mariner 10*. Launched in 1973, it passed close by Venus. It flew 5800 kilometres (3600 miles) above Venus's clouds. While there, it measured wind speeds and temperature. It found that high clouds on Venus looked just like clouds on the Earth.

Until *Mariner 10*, no other space probe had ever been to Mercury. *Mariner 10* flew past Mercury three times before it ran out of fuel. Cameras on

Mariner 10 took pictures and used computers to send them back to the Earth.

The pictures showed that the surface of Mercury looks like the Earth's Moon. It has many craters, or bowl-shaped holes. **Meteorites** crashed into Mercury and created these craters.

Magellan

Even after *Mariner 10*, scientists still knew little about Venus. Venus's clouds surrounded the planet and blocked the view of its surface. Scientists needed a special kind of space probe to see the whole surface.

Two spacecraft from the **Soviet Union** dropped instruments on balloons into Venus's atmosphere in 1985. Four years later, the USA sent the *Magellan* space probe to Venus. *Magellan* carried a radar machine. Radar bounces radio waves off a surface. Radio waves are a form of energy that can travel through clouds.

Magellan used radar to map 98 per cent of the surface of Venus. It sent radio waves downwards and then caught them when they bounced back. The waves told scientists how far down the surface was and how the land was shaped. Scientists found thousands of volcanoes on Venus.

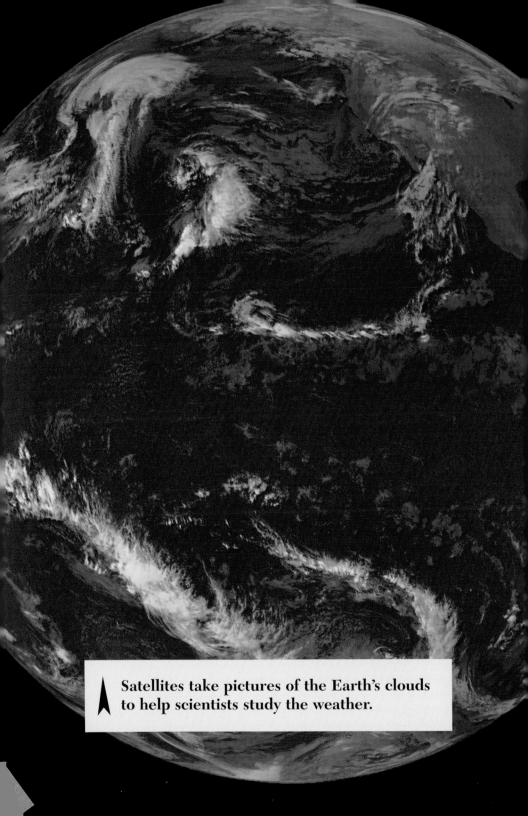

Satellites take pictures of the Earth's clouds
to help scientists study the weather.

Artificial Earth satellites

People cannot see much of the Earth at one time because they live on its surface. Many artificial **satellites** have been sent into orbit above the Earth to give people a better view. Each satellite has a specific job. Some satellites take pictures or record information about the Earth. Other satellites send TV, mobile phone or radio signals around the planet.

Weather satellites take pictures of the Earth's clouds. Meteorologists look at these pictures. Meteorologists are scientists who study the weather. The pictures help them predict the weather. For example, swirling clouds over the Atlantic Ocean warn of a hurricane.

The European Space Agency

The European Space Agency (ESA) has been working since 1975 to develop Europe's future in space. It has fifteen member states in Europe. So far, the ESA has developed a number of satellites, as well as rockets and rocket launchers.

The ESA's astronauts have taken part in four missions to the International Space Station – a huge laboratory in space. An ESA mission planned for 2004 aims to add a robotic arm to the International Space station.

Mars is millions of kilometres away from the Earth. Many space missions failed to reach it.

Flights to Mars

Mars is about 56 million kilometres (35 million miles) away from the Earth at the closest point in its **orbit**. The surface of Mars looks fuzzy even through very powerful telescopes. Scientists must send space probes to Mars to see what the planet really looks like. The space probes send pictures of Mars back to scientists on the Earth.

More than thirty spacecraft have been sent to Mars. Only about half of those survived the trip there.

Mars 1 was the first US space probe scientists tried to send to Mars. On November 1, 1962, *Mars 1* took off from the **Soviet Union**. Scientists lost radio contact with the spacecraft and the mission failed.

In 1964, scientists in the USA tried to send a space probe to Mars. *Mariner 3* had problems, too. It also failed to reach Mars.

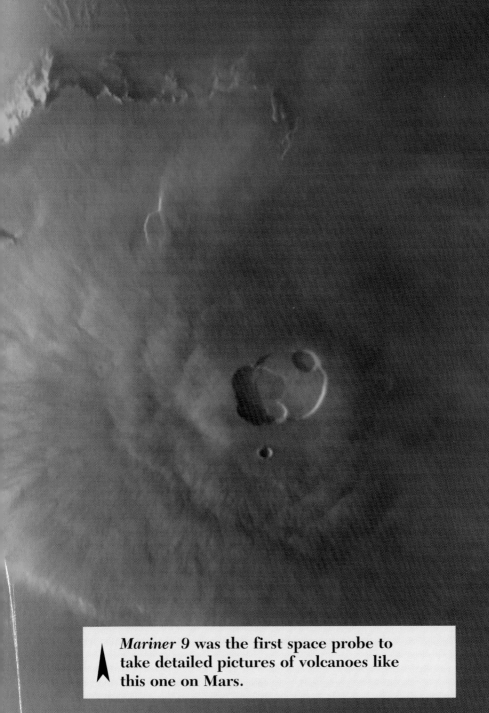

Mariner 9 was the first space probe to take detailed pictures of volcanoes like this one on Mars.

Successful *Mariner* missions

On 28 November 1964, NASA scientists launched the *Mariner 4* spacecraft. This mission was a success. It flew past Mars on 15 July 1965. As it passed the planet, it took many close-up pictures of the surface.

Two more US spacecraft made the trip to Mars in 1969. *Mariner 6* took 75 pictures of Mars. *Mariner 7* took 126 pictures.

The USA sent *Mariner 9* to **orbit** Mars in 1971. When it began orbiting, a big dust storm covered the surface of Mars. *Mariner 9* could only take pictures of the dust clouds.

Over time, the dust storm stopped. The spacecraft began taking more pictures as soon as the dust cleared. *Mariner 9* discovered many features on Mars. It took pictures of deep valleys and giant volcanoes. It found channels on Mars that looked like dried-up streams or rivers. *Mariner 9* also took pictures of marks left on the surface by strong windstorms.

The pictures from the *Mariner* missions helped **astronomers** learn what the surface of Mars looks like. Astronomers also studied the *Mariner* pictures to find places to land future spacecraft.

> **This picture from *Viking* shows the rocks and the orange-pink sky of Mars.**

Viking space probes

The USA launched two spacecraft to Mars in 1975.
These spacecraft were *Viking 1* and *Viking 2*. Each
Viking spacecraft had two parts. The first part was a
large spacecraft built to **orbit** Mars. The second part
was a lander. The lander was built to drop down
from the orbiting spacecraft and land on the surface
of Mars. The *Viking* missions were the first to place
landers on Mars.

The *Viking* spacecraft began to orbit Mars in 1976. They took pictures of Mars and sent them back to the Earth. Scientists looked at the pictures and found places for the landers to touch down. Mission controllers released the landers one month after the spacecraft began to orbit. Mission controllers operate spacecraft from the Earth.

The landers fell towards Mars. They landed just over a month apart and 6440 kilometres (4000 miles) away from each other.

Each *Viking* lander had two cameras that took pictures and sent them back to the Earth. The landers had instruments to check the weather and the soil on Mars. They had machines to measure any movement, such as earthquakes, on the surface of Mars.

Each lander also had a robotic arm. Mission controllers sent commands from the Earth to the lander. The landers did what the controllers instructed. They used their robotic arms to scoop up Martian soil. The *Viking* landers checked the soil for living things. Scientists disagree about the results of the *Viking* tests. Some believe there were signs of life, while others do not think there were any.

Sojourner studied rocks and soil samples on Mars.

Mars *Pathfinder*

In 1997, the USA sent *Pathfinder* into space. *Pathfinder* carried a rover called *Sojourner*. The rover was a small robot car. Scientists sent instructions to *Sojourner* from the Earth.

Pathfinder landed on Mars on 4 July 1997. Huge bags filled with air and surrounded the spacecraft when it landed. *Pathfinder* bounced about fifteen times when it hit the surface. The airbags protected the spacecraft during this bumpy landing.

After *Pathfinder* stopped moving, mission controllers let the air out of the bags. *Pathfinder's* instruments began measuring the weather. Its cameras sent pictures back to the Earth.

Scientists steered *Sojourner* on to Mars. It carried tools to study rocks. *Sojourner* and *Pathfinder* worked for about 85 days until they ran out of power. Scientists are still studying the information they gathered.

Mars Express

The European Space Agency (ESA) plan to send *Mars Express* to Mars in 2003. *Mars Express* will look for hidden water or ice. It will also drop a lander to look for signs of life. The ESA hope it will be the most detailed study of Mars yet.

Visiting the outer solar system

Four giant planets **orbit** far from the Sun in the outer **solar system**. Jupiter, Saturn, Uranus and Neptune are millions of kilometres away from the Sun. It takes special explorer space probes to reach these planets.

The outer solar system is so far away that a rocket would not be able to carry the space probes far enough. The rocket would run out of fuel long before it reached these planets.

Scientists use a planet's **gravity** to help steer the space probes. When a probe comes close to a planet, the planet's gravity pulls on it. This speeds up the probe. It also pulls the probe into a path that curves around the planet. Scientists use this curving to change a space probe's path. That way, the space probe can visit other planets.

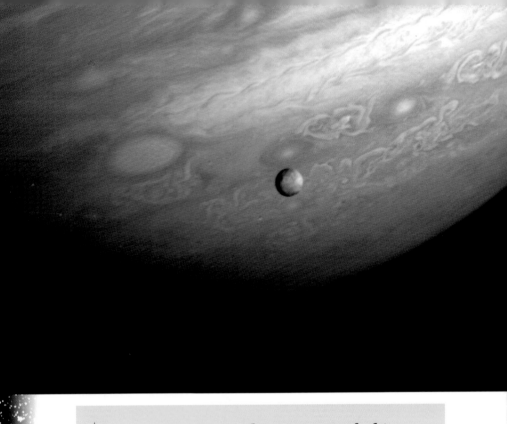

Pioneer missions

In 1972 and 1973, **NASA** launched the *Pioneer 10* and *Pioneer 11* space probes. These probes flew near Jupiter in December 1973 and December 1974. They were the first space probes to fly past Jupiter. *Pioneer 10* then continued on its way out of the solar system. In 1983, it became the first spacecraft sent beyond the solar system. *Pioneer 11* flew past Saturn in September 1979.

Voyager space probes

In 1977, US scientists launched the *Voyager 1* and *Voyager 2* space probes. Each *Voyager* spacecraft has a large dish-shaped **antenna**. Below the antenna is a box that carries scientific instruments. Each spacecraft has two television cameras and tools for measuring temperatures. They also have antennae for sending information to the Earth. The spacecraft have special batteries that are designed to provide power for many years. Each *Voyager* also has small rockets to change its course.

It took the *Voyager* probes almost two years of travelling to reach Jupiter. They visited Jupiter in 1979. They passed the giant planet, taking pictures and measurements. Jupiter's gravity redirected the probes. They were sent into space towards Saturn. They circled Saturn and took pictures. Then *Voyager 1* flew by some of Saturn's moons to take close-up pictures. *Voyager 2* travelled from Saturn to Uranus and then on to Neptune.

The *Voyager* probes are now on their way out of the solar system. As long as they work, the probes will continue to send information about deep space to the Earth. Scientists expect both *Voyagers* to continue working until 2030. At that time, they will run out of power.

Voyager discoveries

Scientists learned many things by studying information from the *Voyager* spacecraft. These space probes gave scientists their first close-up view of Jupiter, Saturn, Uranus and Neptune.

Scientists learned that hurricane-like storms swirl in Jupiter's **atmosphere**. They discovered that different coloured clouds circling the planet give Jupiter its striped appearance. The probes found three faint rings around Jupiter. They also found erupting volcanoes on Jupiter's moon Io.

Voyager 1 flew past Saturn in 1980 and *Voyager 2* passed by in 1981. The probes took pictures of Saturn's rings. The rings look solid from the Earth, but close-up pictures showed that the rings are made of tiny bits of rock, ice and dust. The large rings are made up of thousands of small rings. They look like the lines on a compact disc.

Voyager 2 flew past Uranus in 1986. It found several moons **orbiting** the planet. In 1989, *Voyager 2* flew past Neptune. It took pictures of Neptune and observed a large storm with swirling winds. It studied one of Neptune's moons Triton and found that it is one of the coldest places in the solar system.

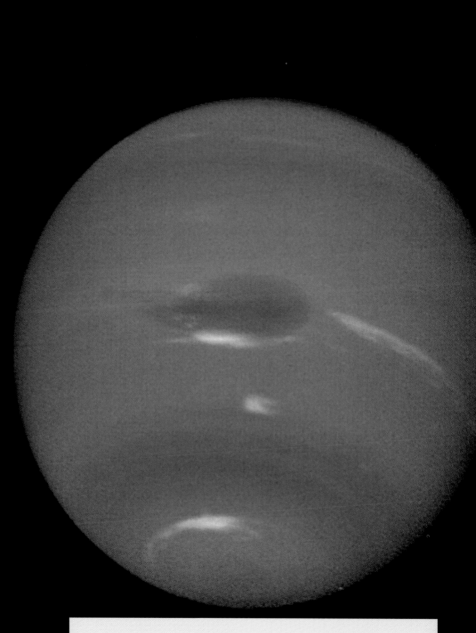

Voyager 2 took this picture of a giant storm on Neptune. The storm looks like a dark spot.

In this picture, astronauts are working on the Hubble Space Telescope.

Deep space

No space probe has ever been to the planet Pluto, the furthest planet from the Sun. A mission is planned for 2006. The Pluto-Kuiper Belt Mission space probe will pass Pluto and Charon in 2015. In 2026 it will pass The Kuiper Belt – a collection of icy objects just beyond Neptune's orbit.

Some telescopes that have already studied Pluto are attached to spacecraft. The Hubble Space Telescope is a telescope that **orbits** the Earth. Hubble looks at objects using light. Other explorer spacecraft take pictures by using energy rays that are invisible to people. For example, the Chandra **X-ray** Observatory looks at objects using X-rays. Other spacecraft use radio waves to study objects in space.

The Hubble Space Telescope took this picture of a distant galaxy.

Distant objects

Telescopes on spacecraft examine deep space. Objects in deep space appear unclear in telescopes on the Earth. This is because the Earth's hazy **atmosphere** blocks and distorts some of the light.

Objects in deep space are also hard to see because they are so far away from the Earth. The nearest star to our Sun is billions of kilometres away. Most objects in space are even further away.

Space telescopes are making many new discoveries. They have found stars of all sizes and colours. Some stars have planets that orbit them.

Scientists have found many new groups of stars using space telescopes. Sometimes a group is only a few dozen stars. Other times, thousands or even millions of stars cluster together. A galaxy is a very large system of stars and objects that orbit the stars. **Gravity** holds the galaxy together. The Earth and the Sun are part of the Milky Way galaxy. This galaxy has more than 100 billion stars.

Scientists use telescopes to study how planets and stars form. These objects form in colourful clouds of gas and dust called nebulas. Telescopes also watch how stars die. By studying this information, scientists are learning about how our **solar system** formed and what the future of the Earth may be.

This is an artist's idea of what the Hugens probe will look like as it lands on Titan.

Future explorers

Each time an explorer space probe visits a planet, scientists make new discoveries but raise new questions. New spacecraft are needed to gather more information so scientists can answer their questions.

Some new spacecraft are already on their way to the gas giants. The *Cassini* spacecraft is travelling to Saturn. It is carrying a small capsule called the Huygens probe that will land on Saturn's moon Titan. The *Messenger* spacecraft is being developed to go to Mercury. It will be the first spacecraft to visit Mercury since *Mariner 10* in 1974.

The European Space Agency (ESA) is planning to build six new space telescopes. The telescopes will work together to scan the nearby universe, looking for signs of Earth-like planets. The ESA have called this mission *Darwin* and hope to launch it in 2015.

Scientists are also planning new missions for astronauts. They are working on ways to send humans to Mars. Some people believe the first human explorers on Mars may arrive there in the next 20 or 30 years. As long as there are questions about space, people will try to explore it.

Glossary

astronomer scientist who studies objects in space

antenna (an-TEN-ah) dish-shaped aerial for sending
  and receiving radio waves

atmosphere layer of gases that surrounds an object
  in space

gravity force that attracts all objects to each other; the
  gravitational force exerted by an object depends on
  its mass

hydrogen the simplest element in the universe;
  hydrogen is an odourless gas

meteorite (ME-tee-or-ite) piece of rock and metal that
  crashes into objects in space

missile rocket that carries a weapon, spacecraft, or
  other payload

orbit path an object takes around another object in
  space

satellite spacecraft sent into space to circle the Earth;
  some satellites take pictures or record information
  about the Earth

solar system the Sun and all the objects that orbit it

Soviet Union country that is now called the Russian
  Federation

X-ray a kind of energy wave that can pass through
  solid bodies

Further information

Websites
BBC Science
http://www.bbc.co.uk/science/space/
British National Space Centre
http://www.bnsc.gov.uk/
European Space Agency
http://sci.esa.int/
**Star Child: A Learning Centre for
    Young Astronomers**
http://starchild.gsfc.nasa.gov/

Books
Exploring the Solar System: The Moon,
    Giles Sparrow (Heinemann Library, 2002)
Take Off!: Space Travel, Jenny Tesar
    (Heinemann Library, 2000)

Useful addresses
London Planetarium   The Science Museum
Marylebone Road   Exhibition Road
London NW1 5LR   London SW7 2DD

Index

Robert H. Goddard

American scientist Robert H. Goddard is nicknamed the 'father of rocket technology'. In the early 1900s, he made many changes and improvements to rocket design. He wanted to create rockets that were powerful enough to carry astronauts to the Moon.

Goddard changed the type of fuel used in rockets. Early rockets all used solid fuel, but Goddard believed that liquid fuel could provide